Daily
Adhkars

Authentic Supplications for Everyday Protection and Blessings of Allah

Dr. Mariam T.

List of Contents

In the name of Allah the Entirely Merciful,
the Especially Merciful.
I seek refuge with Allah from the accursed Shaytan

**Why is Adkhar, Dua, and reading verses of
the Quran daily important for all?**

Allah answers for this question in the Quran

The Qur'an says in Surah Az Zukhruf:

"If anyone withdraws himself from the
remembrance of The Most Gracious, We
appoint for him a Shaytaan, to be an intimate
companion." (Az-Zukhruf, 43:36)

Allahu Akbar
Allah is the Greatest

1. La illaha ilalala, Anta Subhanaka, Inni kuntu
   minadhalimeen. *100 times per day*

   There is no deity except You; exalted are You.

   Indeed, I have been of the wrongdoer

2. Subhan-Allahi wa bihamdihi,

   adada khalqihi,

   Wa rida nafsihi, *3 Times repeat equals 15 hours*

   Wa zinatah `arshihi, *of ibadath*

   Wa midada kalimatihi

   Glory be Allah who is perfect and praise be to Him,

   equal to the magnitude of his creation,

   equal to the weight of His throne,

   equal to His good pleasure and

   equal to the ink that may be used to record His

   words.

2

3. Subhan-Allahi wa bihamdihi,

Subhanallahil Azeem

Glory be Allah who is perfect and praise be to Him,

Glory be to Allah the great 100 times per day

4. Subhan-Allahi   Glory be to Allah

Alhumdulillah   Praise be Allah

Allahu Akbar   Allah is the Greatest

33 times each per day

La ilaha illallahu wahdahu la sharika lahu lahul mulku

wa lahul hamdu wa huwa ala kulli shay in qadeer

None has the right to be worshipped but Allah, the
Alone Who has no partners, to Him belongs Dominion
and to Him belong all the Praises, and He has power
over all things (i.e. Omnipotent)

5. Astagfirullah — I seek Forgiveness from Allah

100 times per day

6. *Syed-ul-Istighfar*

The best supplication for seeking forgiveness

Allahumma anta rabbi laaa ilaaha illa anta. Khalaq tani wa aana a'bduk. Wa aana aa-la ahdika wa wa'di-ka masta-ta'tu. Aa u'zubika min-sharimaa sa-na'tu. Aa-bu u-laka bi-ni'matika a'laiya. Wa aa-bu u-bi-zambi Fagh-firli Fa-inna-hu la yagh-firuz-zu-nu ba il-la anta.

O Allah, You are my Lord, none has the right to be worshipped except You, You created me and I am Your servant, and I abide to Your covenant and promise [to honour it] as best I can, I take refuge in You from the evil of which I committed, I acknowledge Your favour upon me and I acknowledge my sin, so forgive me, for verily none can forgive sins except You.

Ruqyah

The Verses of the Qur'an with which to Repel the effect of Black Magic and all kinds of harm.

Ruqyah' is the practice of treating illnesses through Qur'ānic āyāt and'
invocations as prescribed by the Messenger of Allah ﷺ

The Verses of the Qur'an with Which to Repeal the Effect of Magic

7. *Surah Al Fatihah*

"I seek refuge with Allah from the accursed Shaytan. In the name of Allah the Entirely Merciful, the Especially Merciful."

1. In the name of Allah, Most Gracious, Most Merciful.
2. Praise be to Allah, the Cherisher and Sustainer of the worlds;
3. Most Gracious, Most Merciful;
4. Master of the Day of Judgment.
5. Thee do we worship, and Thine aid we seek.
6. Show us the straight way,
7. The way of those on whom Thou hast bestowed Thy Grace, those whose [portion]is not wrath, and who go not astray.

The Verses of the Qur'an with Which to Repeal the Effect of Magic

7.1 *Surah Al Fatihah (Transliteration)*

1. Bismillaahir Rahmaanir Raheem

2. Alhamdu lillaahi Rabbil 'aalameen

3. Ar-Rahmaanir-Raheem

4. Maaliki Yawmid-Deen

5. Iyyaaka na'budu wa Iyyaaka nasta'een

6. Ihdinas-Siraatal-Mustaqeem

7. Siraatal-lazeena an'amta 'alaihim ghayril-maghdoobi 'alaihim wa lad-daaalleen

8. *First five verses from Surah Al Baqarah (2: 1-5)*

"I seek refuge with Allah from the accursed Shaytan. In the name of Allah the Entirely Merciful, the Especially Merciful."

1. A. L. M.

2. This is the Book; in it is guidance sure, without doubt, to those who fear Allah;

3. Who believe in the Unseen, are steadfast in prayer, and spend out of what We have provided for them;

4. And who believe in the Revelation sent to thee, and sent before thy time, and [in their hearts] have the assurance of the Hereafter.

5. They are on [true] guidance, from their Lord, and it is these who will prosper.

8.1 *First five verses from Surah Al Baqarah (2: 1-5) Transliteration*

Bismillaahir Rahmaanir Raheem

1. Alif-Laaam-Meeem
2. Zaalikal Kitaabu laa raiba feeh; hudal lilmuttaqeen
3. Allazeena yu'minoona bilghaibi wa yuqeemoonas salaata wa mimmaa razaqnaahum yunfiqoon
4. Wallazeena yu'minoona bimaa unzila ilaika wa maaa unzila min qablika wa bil Aakhirati hum yooqinoon
5. Ulaaa'ika 'alaa hudam mir rabbihim wa ulaaa'ika humul muflihoon

9. *Ayat al Kursi (Surah Al Baqarah, 2:255)*

"I seek refuge with Allah from the accursed Shaytan. In the name of Allah the Entirely Merciful, the Especially Merciful."

- 255. Allah! There is no god but He,-the Living, the Self-subsisting, Eternal. No slumber can seize Him nor sleep. His are all things in the heavens and on earth. Who is there can intercede in His presence except as He permitteth? He knoweth what [appeareth to His creatures as] before or after or behind them. Nor shall they compass aught of His knowledge except as He willeth. His Throne doth extend over the heavens and the earth, and He feeleth no fatigue in guarding and preserving them for He is the Most High, the Supreme [in glory].

9.1 *Ayat al Kursi (Surah Al Baqarah, 2:255)*

Trasliteration

Bismillaahir Rahmaanir Raheem

- 255. Allahu laaa ilaaha illaa Huwal Haiyul Qaiyoom; laa taakhuzuhoo sinatunw wa laa nawm; lahoo maa fissamaawaati wa maa fil ard; man zal lazee yashfa'u indahooo illaa bi-iznih; ya'lamu maa baina aydeehim wa maa khalfahum wa laa yuheetoona bishai'im min 'ilmihee illaa bimaa shaaa'; wasi'a Kursiyyuhus samaawaati wal' arda wa laa Ya'ooduhoo hifzuhumaa; wa Huwal Aliyyul 'Azeem

10. *Last two verses from Surah Al Baqarah (2:285)*

"I seek refuge with Allah from the accursed Shaytan. In the name of Allah the Entirely Merciful, the Especially Merciful."

- 285. The Messenger believeth in what hath been revealed to him from his Lord, as do the men of faith. Each one [of them] believeth in Allah, His angels, His books, and His messengers. "We make no distinction [they say] between one and another of His messengers." And they say: "We hear, and we obey: [We seek] Thy forgiveness, our Lord, and to Thee is the end of all journeys."

- "286. On no soul doth Allah Place a burden greater than it can bear. It gets every good that it earns, and it suffers every ill that it earns. [Pray:] "Our Lord! Condemn us not if we forget or fall into error; our Lord! Lay not on us a burden Like that which Thou didst lay on those before us; Our Lord! Lay not on us a burden greater than we have strength to bear. Blot out our sins, and grant us forgiveness. Have mercy on us. Thou art our Protector; Help us against those who stand against faith."

10.1 *Last two verses from Surah Al Baqarah (2:285) Transliteration*

Bismillaahir Rahmaanir Raheem

- 285. Aamanar-Rasoolu bimaaa unzila ilaihi mir-Rabbihee walmu'minoon; kullun aamana billaahi wa Malaaa'ikathihee wa Kutubhihee wa Rusulihee laa nufarriqu baina ahadim-mir-Rusulih wa qaaloo sami'naa wa ata'naa ghufraanaka Rabbanaa wa ilaikal-maseer

- 286. Laa yukalliful-laahu nafsan illaa wus'ahaa; lahaa maa kasabat wa 'alaihaa maktasabat; Rabbanaa laa tu'aakhiznaaa in naseenaaa aw akhtaanaa; Rabbanaa wa laa tahmil-'alainaaa isran kamaa hamaltahoo 'alal-lazeena min qablinaa; Rabbanaa wa laa tuhammil-naa maa laa taaqata lanaa bih; wa'fu 'annaa waghfir lanaa warhamnaa; Anta mawlaanaa fansurnaa 'alal qawmil kaafireen

11. *First five verses from Surah 'Ali 'Imran (3: 1-5)*

"I seek refuge with Allah from the accursed Shaytan. In the name of Allah the Entirely Merciful, the Especially Merciful."

1. Alif, Lam, Mim.

2. Allah! There is no god but He,-the Living, the Self-Subsisting, Eternal.

3. It is He Who sent down to thee [step by step], in truth, the Book, confirming what went before it; and He sent down the Law [of Moses] and the Gospel [of Jesus] before this, as a guide to mankind, and He sent down the criterion [of judgment between right and wrong].

4. Then those who reject Faith in the Signs of Allah will suffer the severest penalty, and Allah is Exalted in Might, Lord of Retribution.

5. From Allah, verily nothing is hidden on earth or in the heavens.

11.1 *First five verses from Surah 'Ali 'Imran (3: 1-5) Transliteration*

Bismillaahir Rahmaanir Raheem

1. Alif-Laam-Meeem

2. Allaahu laaa ilaaha illaa Huwal Haiyul Qaiyoom

3. Nazzala 'alaikal Kitaaba bilhaqqi musaddiqal limaa baina yadaihi wa anzalat Tawraata wal Injeel

4. Min qablu hudal linnaasi wa anzalal Furqaan; innallazeena kafaroo bi Aayaatil laahi lahum 'azaabun shadeed; wallaahu 'azeezun zun tiqaam

5. Innal laaha laa yakhfaa 'alaihi shai'un fil ardi wa laa fis samaaa'

12. *Verses 54, 55, and 56 from Surah Al 'A'raf (7: 54-56)*

"I seek refuge with Allah from the accursed Shaytan. In the name of Allah the Entirely Merciful, the Especially Merciful."

- 54. Your Guardian-Lord is Allah, Who created the heavens and the earth in six days, and is firmly established on the throne [of authority]: He draweth the night as a veil o'er the day, each seeking the other in rapid succession: He created the sun, the moon, and the stars, [all] governed by laws under His command. Is it not His to create and to govern? Blessed be Allah, the Cherisher and Sustainer of the worlds!

"I seek refuge with Allah from the accursed Shaytan. In the name of Allah the Entirely Merciful, the Especially Merciful."

- 55. Call on your Lord with humility and in private: for Allah loveth not those who trespass beyond bounds.

- 56. Do no mischief on the earth, after it hath been set in order, but call on Him with fear and longing [in your hearts]: for the Mercy of Allah is [always] near to those who do good.

12.1 *Verses 54, 55, and 56 from Surah Al 'A'raf (7: 54-56) Transliteration*

Bismillaahir Rahmaanir Raheem

- 54. Inna Rabbakumul laahul lazee khalaqas samaawaati wal arda fee sittati ayyaamin summas tawaa 'alal 'arshi yughshil lailan nahaara yatlu buhoo haseesanw washshamsa walqamara wannujooma musakharaatim bi amrih; alaa lahul khalqu wal-amr; tabaarakal laahu Rabbul 'aalameen

- 55. Ud'oo Rabbakum tadarru'anw wa khufyah; innahoo laa yuhibbul mu'tadeen

- 56. Wa laa tufsidoo fil ardi ba'da islaahihaa wad'oohu khawfanw wa tama'aa; inna rahmatal laahi qareebum minal muhsineen

13. *Verses 117, 118, and 119 from Surah Al 'A'raf* *(7: 117-119)*

"I seek refuge with Allah from the accursed Shaytan. In the name of Allah the Entirely Merciful, the Especially Merciful."

- 117. We put it into Moses's mind by inspiration: "Throw [now] thy rod": and behold! it swallows up straight away all the falsehoods which they fake!
- 118. Thus truth was confirmed, and all that they did was made of no effect.
- 119. So the [great ones] were vanquished there and then, and were made to look small.

Bismillaahir Rahmaanir Raheem

- 117. Wa awhainaaa ilaa Moosaaa an alqi 'asaaka fa izaa hiya talqafu maa ya'fikoon
- 118. Fawaqa'al haqqu wa batala maa kaanoo ya'maloon
- 119. Faghuliboo hunaalika wanqalaboo saaghireen

14. *Verses 79, 80, 81, and 82 from Surah Yunus (10: 79-82)*

"I seek refuge with Allah from the accursed Shaytan. In the name of Allah the Entirely Merciful, the Especially Merciful."

- 79. Said Pharaoh: "Bring me every sorcerer well versed."
- 80. When the sorcerers came, Moses said to them: "Throw ye what ye [wish] to throw!"
- 81. When they had had their throw, Moses said: "What ye have brought is sorcery: Allah will surely make it of no effect: for Allah prospereth not the work of those who make mischief.
- 82. "And Allah by His words doth prove and establish His truth, however much the sinners may hate it!"

14.1 *Verses 79, 80, 81, and 82 from Surah Yunus (10: 79-82) Transliteration*

Bismillaahir Rahmaanir Raheem

- 79. Wa qaala Fir'awnu' toonee bikulli saahirin 'aleem
- 80. Falammaa jaaa'assa haratu qaala lahum Moosaaa alqoo maaa antum mulqoon
- 81. Falammaaa alqaw qaala Moosaa maa ji'tum bihis sihr; innal laaha sa yubtiluhoo; innal laaha laa yuslihu 'amalal mufsideen
- 82. Wa yuhiqqul laahul haqqa bi Kalimaatihee wa law karihal mujrimoon

"I seek refuge with Allah from the accursed Shaytan. In the name of Allah the Entirely Merciful, the Especially Merciful."

- 65. They said: "O Moses! whether wilt thou that thou throw [first] or that we be the first to throw?"

- 66. He said, "Nay, throw ye first!" Then behold their ropes and their rods-so it seemed to him on account of their magic - began to be in lively motion!

- 67. So Moses conceived in his mind a [sort of] fear.

- 68. We said: "Fear not! for thou hast indeed the upper hand:

- 69. "Throw that which is in thy right hand: Quickly will it swallow up that which they have faked what they have faked is but a magician's trick: and the magician thrives not, [no matter] where he goes."

15.1 *Verses 65, 66, 67, 68, and 69 from Surah Taha (20: 65-69) Transliteration*

Bismillaahir Rahmaanir Raheem

- 65. Qaaloo yaa Moosaaa immaaa an tulqiya wa immaaa an nakoona awala man alqaa
- 66. Qaala bal alqoo fa izaa hibaaluhum wa 'isiyyuhum yukhaiyalu ilaihi min sihrihim annahaa tas'aa
- 67. Fa awjasa fee nafsihee kheefatam Moosa
- 68. Qulnaa laa takhaf innaka antal a'laa
- 69. Wa alqi maa fee yamee nika talqaf maa sana'oo; innamaa sana'oo kaidu saahir; wa laa yuflihus saahiru haisu ataa

16. *Verses 115, 116, 117, and 118 from Surah Al Mu'minun* *(23: 115-118)*

"I seek refuge with Allah from the accursed Shaytan. In the name of Allah the Entirely Merciful, the Especially Merciful."

- 115. "Did ye then think that We had created you in jest, and that ye would not be brought back to Us [for account]?"

- 116. Therefore exalted be Allah, the King, the Reality: there is no god but He, the Lord of the Throne of Honour!

- 117. If anyone invokes, besides Allah, Any other god, he has no authority therefor; and his reckoning will be only with his Lord! and verily the Unbelievers will fail to win through!

- 118. So say: "O my Lord! grant Thou forgiveness and mercy for Thou art the Best of those who show mercy!"

16.1 *Verses 115, 116, 117, and 118 from Surah Al Mu'minun (23: 115-118) Transliteration*

Bismillaahir Rahmaanir Raheem

- 115. Afahasibtum annamaa khalaqnaakum 'abasanw wa annakum ilainaa laa turja'oon
- 116. Fata'alal laahul Malikul Haqq; laaa ilaaha illaa Huwa Rabbul 'Arshil Kareem
- 117. Wa mai yad'u ma'allaahi ilaahan aakhara laa burhaana lahoo bihee fa inna maa hisaabuhoo 'inda Rabbih; innahoo laa yuflihul kaafiroon
- 118. Wa qul Rabbigh fir warham wa Anta khairur raahimeen

17. *First ten verses from Surah As Saffat (37: 1-10)*

"I seek refuge with Allah from the accursed Shaytan. In the name of Allah the Entirely Merciful, the Especially Merciful."

1. By those who range themselves in ranks,

2. And so are strong in repelling [evil],

3. And thus proclaim the Message [of Allah]!

4. Verily, verily, your Allah is one!-

5. Lord of the heavens and of the earth and all between them, and Lord of every point at the rising of the sun!

6. We have indeed decked the lower heaven with beauty [in] the stars,-

7. [For beauty] and for guard against all obstinate rebellious evil spirits,

8. [So] they should not strain their ears in the direction of the Exalted Assembly but be cast away from every side,

9. Repulsed, for they are under a perpetual penalty,

10. Except such as snatch away something by stealth, and they are pursued by a flaming fire, of piercing brightness.

17.1 *First ten verses from Surah As Saffat (37: 1-10) Transliteration*

Bismillaahir Rahmaanir Raheem

1. Wassaaaffaati saffaa
2. Fazzaajiraati zajraa
3. Fattaaliyaati Zikra
4. Inna Illaahakum la Waahid
5. Rabbus samaawaati wal ardi wa maa bainahumaa wa Rabbul mashaariq
6. Innaa zaiyannas samaaa 'ad dunyaa bizeenatinil kawaakib
7. Wa hifzam min kulli Shaitaanim maarid
8. Laa yassamma 'oona ilal mala 'il a'alaa wa yuqzafoona min kulli jaanib
9. Duhooranw wa lahum 'azaabunw waasib
10. Illaa man khatifal khatfata fa atba'ahoo shihaabun saaqib

18. *Verses 21, 22, 23, and 24 from Surah Al Hashr (59: 21-24)*

"I seek refuge with Allah from the accursed Shaytan. In the name of Allah the Entirely Merciful, the Especially Merciful."

- 21. Had We sent down this Qur'an on a mountain, verily, thou wouldst have seen it humble itself and cleave asunder for fear of Allah. Such are the similitudes which We propound to men, that they may reflect.

- 22. Allah is He, than Whom there is no other god;- Who knows [all things] both secret and open; He, Most Gracious, Most Merciful.

- 23. Allah is He, than Whom there is no other god;- the Sovereign, the Holy One,the Source of Peace [and Perfection], the Guardian of Faith, the Preserver of Safety, the Exalted in Might, the Irresistible, the Supreme: Glory to Allah! [High is He] above the partners they attribute to Him.

- 24. He is Allah, the Creator, the Evolver, the Bestower of Forms [or Colours]. To Him belong the Most Beautiful Names: whatever is in the heavens and on earth, doth declare His Praises and Glory: and He is the Exalted in Might, the Wise.

18.1 *Verses 21, 22, 23, and 24 from Surah Al Hashr (59: 21-24) Transliteration*

Bismillaahir Rahmaanir Raheem

- 21. Law anzalnaa haazal quraana 'alaa jabilil lara aytahoo khaashi'am muta saddi'am min khashiyatil laah; wa tilkal amsaalu nadribuhaa linnaasi la'allahum yatafakkaroon
- 22. Huwal-laahul-lazee laaa Ilaaha illaa Huwa 'Aalimul Ghaibi wash-shahaada; Huwar Rahmaanur-Raheem
- 23. Huwal-laahul-lazee laaa Ilaaha illaa Huwal-Malikul Quddoosus-Salaamul Muminul Muhaiminul-'aAzeezul Jabbaarul-Mutakabbir; Subhaanal laahi 'Ammaa yushrikoon
- 24. Huwal Laahul Khaaliqul Baari 'ul Musawwir; lahul Asmaaa'ul Husnaa; yusabbihu lahoo maa fis samaawaati wal ardi wa Huwal 'Azeezul Hakeem

19. *Verses 51 and 52 from Surah Al Qalam (68: 51,52)*

"I seek refuge with Allah from the accursed Shaytan. In the name of Allah the Entirely Merciful, the Especially Merciful."

- 51. And the Unbelievers would almost trip thee up with their eyes when they hear the Message; and they say: "Surely he is possessed!"
- 52. But it is nothing less than a Message to all the worlds.

Transliteration

Bismillaahir Rahmaanir Raheem

- 51. Wa iny-yakaadul lazeena kafaroo la-yuzliqoonaka biabsaarihim lammaa sami'uz-Zikra wa yaqooloona innahoo lamajnoon
- 52. Wa maa huwa illaa zikrul lil'aalameen

20. Surah Al 'Ikhlas (112)

"I seek refuge with Allah from the accursed Shaytan. In the name of Allah the Entirely Merciful, the Especially Merciful."

1. Say: He is Allah, the One and Only;

2. Allah, the Eternal, Absolute;

3. He begetteth not, nor is He begotten;

4. And there is none like unto Him.

Transliteration

3 times per day equals reading entire Quran

Bismillaahir Rahmaanir Raheem

1. Qul huwal laahu ahad

2. Allah hus-samad

3. Lam yalid wa lam yoolad

4. Wa lam yakul-lahoo kufuwan ahad

21. *Surah Al Falaq (113)*

"I seek refuge with Allah from the accursed Shaytan. In the name of Allah the Entirely Merciful, the Especially Merciful."

1. Say: I seek refuge with the Lord of the Dawn
2. From the mischief of created things;
3. From the mischief of Darkness as it overspreads;
4. From the mischief of those who practise secret arts;
5. And from the mischief of the envious one as he practises envy.

21.1 *Surah Al Falaq (113) Transliteration*

Bismillaahir Rahmaanir Raheem

1. Qul a'oozu bi rabbil-falaq

2. Min sharri maa khalaq

3. Wa min sharri ghaasiqin izaa waqab

4. Wa min sharrin-naffaa-saati fil 'uqad

5. Wa min sharri haasidin izaa hasad

22. *Surah An Nas*

"I seek refuge with Allah from the accursed Shaytan. In the name of Allah the Entirely Merciful, the Especially Merciful."

1. Say: I seek refuge with the Lord and Cherisher of Mankind,
2. The King [or Ruler] of Mankind,
3. The god [or judge] of Mankind,-
4. From the mischief of the Whisperer [of Evil], who withdraws [after his whisper],-
5. [The same] who whispers into the hearts of Mankind,-
6. Among Jinns and among men.

Bismillaahir Rahmaanir Raheem

1. Qul a'oozu birabbin naas

2. Malikin naas

3. Ilaahin naas

4. Min sharril waswaasil khannaas

5. Allazee yuwaswisu fee sudoorin naas

6. Minal jinnati wannaas

Ruqyah

Al Ruqyah from the
Prophet's ﷺ Sunnah

Ruqyah' is the practice of treating illnesses through Qur'ānic āyāt and'

invocations as prescribed by the Messenger of Allah ﷺ

Supplications to purify and heal oneself from the troubles of the evil eye

23.

U'eethukumaa bikalimaatillahit-taam-maati min kulli shaiTaaniw-wahaam-maatin wamin kulli 'aynin laam-mah.

"I seek protection for you in the Perfect Words of Allah from every devil and every beast, and from every envious, blameworthy eye." *(Sahih al-Bukhari)*

24.

Bismillaahi arqeeka min kulli shay-in yu'-theeka, min sharri kulli nafsin aw aynin Haasidin Allaahu yashfeeka, bismillaahi arqeek.

"In the Name of Allah I pray over you for healing (Ruqyah), from everything that bothers you, from the evil of every soul and every evil eye that hates you, may Allah cure you, in the Name of Allah I pray over you for healing." *(Muslim)*

25.

Bismillaahi yubreeka wamin kulli daa-in yashfeeka wamin sharri Haasidin ithaa Hasada, wa sharri kulli thee 'ayn.

"In the name of Allah. He may cure you from all kinds of illness and safeguard you from the evil of a jealous one when he feels jealous and from the evil influence of eye." *(Sahih Muslim)*

26.

Allaahumma ath-hibil ba'-sa rabban-naasi ishfi antash-shaafee laa shifaa-a illaa shifaauka shifaa-an laa yughaadiru saqamaa.

"O Allah, Lord of the people, take away the disease and cure him; You are the One Who cures and there is no cure except Your Cure – a cure that leaves no disease." (*Al-Bukhari, Muslim*)

Note: Touch the sick person with the right hand and supplicate the supplication. You can also recite the supplication for yourself.

27.

Bismillaah. A'oothu billaahi wa qudratihee min sharri maa ajidu wa uHaathir.

"In the Name of Allah." (3 times) "I seek refuge in Allah and in His Power from the evil of what I find and of what I guard against. " (7 times) (*Muslim*)

28.

Ibn ʿAbbas (may Allah be pleased with him) reported: The Prophet ﷺ said, "He who visits a sick person who is not on the point of death and supplicates seven times:

أَسْأَلُ اللهَ الْعَظِيمَ، رَبَّ الْعَرْشِ الْعَظِيمِ، أَنْ يَشْفِيَكَ

As-alullaahal 'aDHeema rabbal 'arshil aDHeemi an yashfi-yak.

"I beseech Allah the Great, the Rubb of the Great Throne, to heal you."

Allah will certainly heal him from that sickness." (*Abu Dawud, At-Tirmidhi*)

29.

A'oothu bikalimaatillahit-taam-maati min ghadhabihi wa 'iqaabihi wamin sharri 'ibaadihee wamin hamazaatish-shayaaTeeni wa-an yaHdhuroon.

"I seek refuge with the complete words of Allah from His anger and His punishment and the evil of His slaves, and from the evil suggestions of the shayatin and from their being present (at death)." (*At-Tirmidhi, 3528*)

30.

A'oothu bikalimaatillahit-taam-maati min sharri maa khalaq.

"I seek refuge with the complete words of Allah from the evil of what He has created." (*Muslim, 55*)

31.

Allaahumma innee a'oothu biwajhikal kareemi wa kalimaatikat-taammati min sharri maa anta aakhithum-binaaSiyatih, Allaahumma anta takshiful maghrama wal ma'-tham, Allaahumma laa yuhzamu junduka walaa yukhlafu wa'duka walaa yanfa'u thal jaddi minkal jadd subHaanaka wa bihHamdik.

"O Allah, I seek refuge in Your noble Person and in Your perfect Words from the evil of what You have seized by its forelock; O Allah! You remove debt and sin; O Allah! Your troop is not routed, Your promise is not broken and the riches of the rich do not avail against You. Glory and praise be to You." (*Abu Dawud, 5052*)

32.

Bismillaahil-lathee laa yadhurru ma'asmihi shay-un fil ardhi walaa fis-samaa'.

"In the name of Allah, when Whose name is mentioned nothing on Earth or in Heaven can cause harm." (*Ahmad, 62/1*)

33.

A'oothu bikalimaatillahit-taam-maatil-latee laa yujaawizuhunna barrun walaa faaiirun min sharri maa khalaaa wa thara-a wa bara-a wamin sharri maa yanzilu mins-samaai wamin sharri maa y'ruju feehaa wamin sharri maa thara-a fil ardhi wamin sharri maa yakhruju minhaa wamin sharri fitanil-layli wan-nahaar wamin sharri kulli Taariqin illaa Taariqan yaTruqu bikhayrin yaa raHmaan.

"I seek refuge with the complete words of Allah which neither the good person nor the corrupt can exceed, from the evil of what He has created and originated and multiplied, from the evil of what descends from the sky and the evil of what ascends in it, and from the evil of what is created in the earth and the evil of what comes out of it, and from the trials of the night and day, and from the visitations of the night and day, except for one that knocks with good, O Merciful." *(Ahmad, 419/3)*

34.

Allaahumma rabbas-samaawaati warabbal ardhi warabbal 'arshil aDHeem rabbanaa warabba kulli shayy'-faaliqal Habbi wan-nawaa wa munzilat-tawraati wal injeeli wal furqaan a'oothu bika min sharri kulli shayyin anta aakhithun-

binaaSiyatih allaahumma antal awwalu falaysa qablaka shayyun wa antal aakhiru falaysa ba'daka shayyun wa antaDH-Dhaahir falaysa fawqaka shayyun wa antal baaTinu falaysa doonaka shayy'.

"O Allah, Lord of the heavens and the earth, our Lord and Lord of everything, Who splits the grain and the kernel, Who has sent down the Torah and the Injeel and the Qur'an. I seek refuge in You from the evil of every source of evil whom You do seize by the forelock. O Allah! You are the First, nothing being before You and You are the last, nothing being after You. You are the Manifest, nothing being above You and You are the Hidden, nothing being beyond You." *(Abu Dawud, 5051)*

Supplications for protection and healing

There is nothing wrong with taking precautions against the evil eye before it happens, and this does not contradict the idea of tawakkul (putting one's trust in Allah). In fact this is tawakkul, because tawakkul means putting one's trust in Allah whilst also implementing the means that have been permitted or enjoined. The Prophet ﷺ used to seek refuge for al-Hasan and al-Husayn and say: *U'eethukumaa bikalimaatillahit-taam-maati min kulli shaiTaaniw-wahaam-maatin wamin kulli 'aynin laam-mah* ("I seek refuge for you both in the perfect words of Allah, from every devil and every poisonous reptile, and from every evil eye").'" (*Al-Tirmidhi, 2060; Abu Dawood, 4737*) And he would say, "Thus Ibraheem used to seek refuge with Allah for Ishaaq and Ismaa'eel, peace be upon them both." (*Al-Bukhaari, 3371*)
(*Fataawa al-Shaykh Ibn 'Uthaymeen, 2/117, 118*)

Alhumdulillah.

Dhul Jalali wal ikram,

Malikum Mulk.

Ya Arham ar-rahimeen

Hasibun Allahu Wanimal Wakeel.

All Praise be to Allah

The One Who has all Greatness

You are the Most Merciful of those who show mercy

Sufficient for us is Allah, and [He is] the best Disposer of affairs.

References

- The holy Qur'an - Abdullah Yusuf Ali Translation. Wordsworth Editions, 2000.
- www.quran411.com
- https://sunnah.com/riyadussalihin/16
- https://sunnah.com/bukhari
- https://sunnah.com/muslim

Printed in Great Britain
by Amazon

21025758R00029